Grace
In
the Wilderness

NELSON GIANT PRINT INSPIRATIONAL

Grace In The Wilderness

by
John W. Coffey, Jr.

THOMAS NELSON INC.
NASHVILLE / NEW YORK

Library of Congress Cataloging in Publication Data.

Coffey, John W.
    Grace in the Wilderness.

    "Nelson giant print inspirational."
    1. Sermons, American.   2. Sight-saving books.
I.   Title.
BV4253.C63   252   74–18292
ISBN 0–8407–5579–1

To my
  dear wife,
Helen

Contents

Foreword

During the winter of 1972–1973, a verse from the book of Jeremiah kept weaving through my thoughts: "The people who survived the sword found grace in the wilderness" (Jeremiah 31:2). The phrase, "grace in the wilderness," pressed hard upon me, and I was reminded of the wilderness moments of my own life, and how at those times I seemed to be drawn ever closer to God as he drew near to me. I was in the fifth year of my ministry that winter, and I could see this pattern in others also. As I walked the wilderness with a member of the congregation, I became increasingly aware that God was working his grace in both him and me. In a strange way, he worked the power of his grace in us *together*.

My great hope is that you too will sense the probing, searching grace of God in the wilderness moments of your life, and that you too will be captured and held by this wondrous grace.

JOHN W. COFFEY, JR.
WALKER, MINNESOTA

Grace
In
the Wilderness

Thus says the Lord:
"The people who survived the sword
found grace in the wilderness;
when Israel sought for rest,
the Lord appeared to him from
afar.
I have loved you with an everlasting
love;
therefore I have continued my faith-
fulness to you."

Jeremiah 31:2–3

Grace

In

The Wilderness:

A Prelude

God finds you in the wilderness moments of your life. Or He may not find
you at all.

If you cannot permit God to draw near
to you in the bleak, desolate, desperate
moments of your life, then the likelihood
is quite slim that He will ever capture you
for Himself. Those moments of wilderness, when the soul thirsts for hope
and strength, are the moments that God
monitors carefully. For these are His
great opportunities to move in upon you
and to weave His web of grace into the

fabric of your life. The grace of God comes home most mightily when you welcome Him into the wilderness voids that you experience. Indeed, the pillar of fire — the leading hand of God — shines far brighter, far clearer, in the darkness of your wilderness than in the light of your self-esteem.

And there is wilderness in everyone's life — moments of doubt, times of loneliness, despair, uncertainty, and moral confusion. These are the times when joy, confidence, and certainty collapse, when the soul hungers for understanding, forgiveness, and love. These are not times that you plan; they just happen. You're in a bleak wilderness, and you can give no good reason for being there. The prodigal son had no intention of eating with the pigs when he left his father's home. But there he was, and in the pigpen he came to realize the depth of his father's love.

And so with us. In the wilderness moments of our life, we come to know the depth of God's love, the binding power of His grace.

Now what about this matter of "Grace?" What do we mean when we speak of the "Grace of God?"

Well, it's not something that we do, but rather it's something that God does. The question of the nature of God's grace inevitably leads us to the far greater question of the nature of God himself. It's the grace of God that concerns us here, not some human virtue that some may possess. Grace, as a human characteristic, implies "beauty," "charm," and "attractiveness." This is not what we're dealing with here. Surely, there is a certain beauty, and charm, and attractiveness about God, but the grace of God that breaks through to my wilderness, that finds me in the misery of my lostness, far exceeds some Godly or human virtue. The depth of human misery far exceeds human pity, human sympathy, human grace.

No, in the darkness of his wilderness, a

man needs his God, a God who breaks into the wilderness, who comforts and lifts up, who leads out of the wilderness. And this acting, seeking, leading of God is the Godly grace. Grace is the active element in God's love. He loves, and grace acts. And it acts mightily in the wilderness moments of your life.

And the great clue to the nature of God and His grace is found in this Jesus Christ, who is the living grace of God eternally in our midst. I may look to the stars, the hills, the lakes and in them perceive the order and the beauty of God's handiwork. But neither order nor beauty nor charm are going to reach me in the wilderness hells I encounter. I need hope, not order; certainty, not beauty; strength, not charm. I need God. I need the fulness of his mercy, the fulness of his forgiveness, and the fulness of His steadfast love. In the depths of the wilderness, I am in need of a new creation, a beginning again of closeness to God.

Into the darkness of wilderness comes this Light, Jesus Christ. He comes from God into the deep, dark places of our lives to usher us back to the throne of God. As Christ comes to join us in the wilderness moments, he comes full of grace and truth, and that grace *of* God *in* Christ grips us, holds us, and shapes us. We are shaped by God into sons and heirs — sons by the One Son, heirs by his creative grace.

His creative grace is the life line that leads us out of the wilderness. Then Christ comes; he finds us; and we are more than convinced. We are mastered; we are even more than mastered; we are won — won for God. In the wilderness moments, God seems most able to shape and mold us. For God did not create this earth out of "nothing." He created it out of void and darkness. So it was with the first man. God did not create him out of "nothing." He created him out of the dust of the ground. And God continues to create each day in the same way. Out of the darkness and void and dust of your life, God hovers to create again and again.

So the grace of God flourishes in the desert wilderness. His grace is more of the tough cactus than the delicate rose. In your wilderness moments, the roots of God's grace take on depth and strength. If they don't — if you cannot let God touch you in those desert moments — then *all* is death in the desert.

Now how does this grace work? How can it "happen" in the wilderness moments of your life? Well that is what this book is about. As in all matters of life and faith, we begin with the Word of God, and we will let the Scripture passages lead us through a number of wilderness concerns, and hopefully we will see, by faith, how this wondrous grace of God "happens."

And there he came to a cave, and lodged there; and behold, the word of the Lord came to him, and he said to him, "What are you doing here, Elijah?" He said, "I have been very jealous for the Lord, the God of hosts; for the people of Israel have forsaken thy covenant, thrown down thy altars, and slain thy prophets with the sword; and I, even I only, am left; and they seek my life, to take it away." And he said, "Go forth, and stand upon the mount before the Lord." And behold, the Lord passed by, and a great and strong wind rent the mountains, and broke in pieces the rocks before the Lord, but the Lord was not in the wind; and after the wind an earthquake, but the Lord was not in the earthquake; and after the earthquake a fire, but the Lord was not in the fire; and after the fire a still small voice. And when Elijah heard it, he wrapped his face in his mantle and went out and stood at the entrance of the cave. And behold, there came a voice to him, and said, "What are you doing here, Elijah?" He said, "I have been very jealous for the Lord, the God of hosts; for the people of Israel have forsaken thy covenant, thrown down thy altars, and slain thy prophets with the sword; and I, even I only, am left; and they seek my life, to take it away." And the Lord said to him, "Go, return on your way to the wilderness of Damascus; and when you arrive, you shall anoint Hazael to be king over Syria;. . ."

1 Kings 19:9–15

Grace

In

The Wilderness:

of Loneliness

Loneliness is an awesome wilderness. It's not the aloneness that's so bad, but rather the sense of abandonment that hurts.

We can absorb the alone times. Indeed, moments set apart from the turbulent currents of daily activities can be precious and significant moments. In solitude, we meditate best; we create best; we pray best. In solitude, a sense of peace can steal upon us. We need time alone each day, and we ought to carefully schedule those moments.

But loneliness that grows out of a sense of abandonment is a harsh and lonely wilderness. To be cut off from the sources of love that feed your soul is a bleak solitude. To feel isolated from those who need your love is a bewildering wilderness that appears to offer no exits.

And a choking dust rises out of this wilderness — *the dust of self-pity*. With no one to turn to, we turn inward, searching for whatever sources that will offer hope and comfort. The deeper we probe, the more apparent is our bankruptcy as our search uncovers a conscience that simmers with guilt and fraud. And in this wilderness of loneliness, we feel sorry for ourselves. No one seems to care.

And that is the way it was for Elijah. At Jezebel's threat to take his life, Elijah fled into the wilderness: "But he himself went a day's journey into the wilderness. . ." And there in the wilderness, he withdrew to a cave — alone.

But God had not abandoned Elijah.

"What are you doing here, Elijah?" God asked. And Elijah said, ". . .I, even I only am left; and they seek my life to take it away."

In the isolation of his wilderness cave, Elijah felt sorry for himself. But twice God pressed home the question: "What are you doing here?" Twice Elijah responded with, "I, even I only am left." And then God led Elijah out of his wilderness of loneliness with the word, "Go!" The still small voice of God reached Elijah: "Go forth, and stand upon the mount before the Lord," and "Go, return on your way to the wilderness of Damascus. . ."

God had not abandoned Elijah in that wilderness of Sinai, and the call to go forth, first before the Lord, and then into the wildernessess of others was sounded clearly to Elijah.

Here then is the word to our own moments of loneliness. We begin with the certainty that we are not abandoned by

God; we go forth to the Lord, and we go into the broad world of other people.

The grand message of God to His people is that He has not abandoned us. One of the strong and certain fibers of His grace is that "the dwelling place of God is with men." *Here. Now. Precisely where you happen to be.* The real pit of loneliness is that you feel you have been overlooked and don't count in God's grand scheme of creation.

But God would not have it that way. The central truth of that silent night, that holy night, at Bethlehem is that the eternal God of all creation broke into the affairs of men, to be enrolled on our side. There, in that Jesus of the manger, the still small voice of God sounded among men "full of grace and truth." And on the cross of that Jesus, God poured out His grace, that the smoldering coals of my guilty conscience may be covered over with the forgiveness that God alone can offer. There on the cross, God acted to move me into His house as a son. I am a stranger no more. And the resurrection of this strong Son of God is my certainty that not even in death would God abandon me. Indeed the God who numbers the sparrows, who numbers the hairs of your head, has you eternally on his roster. As the certainty of God's closeness fills your soul, the panic of loneliness eases. You may be alone with God. Those are moments of great communion with God. But with Him, you are never lonely.

Then, certain that at least we count with God, we "go forth and stand upon the mount before the Lord."

And we go forth to the Lord in prayer. Out of the wilderness of our loneliness we lift our voices to God, "our Father who art in heaven." We go forth out of the wilderness on a bridge of prayer. Indeed, prayer makes loneliness bearable; it puts hope in our despair.

And we pray not only because we are sure that God hears us. What father does not hear the words of his children? But we pray also because the prayers that we offer are God's great opportunity to act upon us in his answer. Our prayer is far less *our* bridge to God, but far more is the bridge over which God comes to us. In the words of prayer, God penetrates and captivates the praying soul.

So in our loneliness, we pray. It's our great invitation to God to come and remove the darkness of our loneliness. As we offer our prayers in the wilderness, God moves in upon us, and we become more sure of His grace than our need, more sure of God's closeness than our loneliness. In prayer, our loneliness is taken up by God's nearness.

And then, as did Elijah, we go and return "to the wilderness of Damascus," into the broad world of other people.

In a strange way, the exit out of this wilderness of loneliness is not some mystic leap into the lap of God. Nor are we given the option of holing up·in a cave of self-righteous and self-serving. No, God leads us out of our loneliness as He points us to our brother. *And it's to our brother's wilderness that He leads us.* "Serve him in whatever wilderness he may find himself, and you serve me," God says.

The great problem with loneliness is that you can't share it. *Share it, and you give it up.* Share it, with both God and those around you, and it dissolves in God's grace and your brother's need.

As we venture out of the cave of our own loneliness into the wilderness of our brother, we find that we are in good company. There we find God at work, shaping and gathering a Kingdom. There the Light of the World prowls around in the darkness of every man who will let him. And you move out with him in the certainty that the Risen Christ *meant it* when he said, "Lo, I am with you. . ." As you move into the wilderness of your brother, you converge with God as he works the works of grace in him. There in his wilderness you meet both God *and* your brother, and you come to the realization that God does not give us so much to ourselves, but rather he enables us to give ourselves to Him as well as to those around us. In this network of finding your brother in *his* wilderness, your loneliness gives way to the power of Christian love.

Elijah was found by grace in his loneliness. If that be your wilderness at this moment, let this God of steadfast grace draw near to you, that he may confirm in you the certainty that you are never outside of his love and care. He will call you to prayer, and he will point you to your neighbor.

And the awesome wilderness of your loneliness will be caught up in the wondrous grace of God.

On that day, when evening had come, he said to them, "Let us go across to the other side." And leaving the crowd, they took him with them, just as he was, in the boat. And other boats were with him. And a great storm of wind arose, and the waves beat into the boat so that the boat was already filling. But he was in the stern, asleep on the cushion; and they woke him and said to him, "Teacher, do you not care if we perish?" And he awoke and rebuked the wind, and said to the sea, "Peace! Be still!" And the wind ceased, and there was a great calm. He said to them, "Why are you afraid? Have you no faith?" And they were filled with awe, and said to one another, "Who then is this, that even wind and sea obey him?"

Mark 4:35–41

And Jesus said to him, "if you can! All things are possible to him who believes." Immediately the father of the child cried out and said, "I believe; help my unbelief!"

Mark 9:23–24

Grace

In

The Wilderness:

of Doubt

That we believe in God *at all* is a strange and marvelous thing. Strange, in that the deep commitment of a man to his God does not rise out of the depths of the soul. Marvelous, in that God himself invades the human heart to create that response: "God, I believe." That we believe in God at all is sure and certain evidence that we have been touched by God himself in the Holy Spirit.

But the mere idea of God does not make us religious or Christian. No matter how pure and noble my thoughts may be toward God and about God, they will be of little strength in the stormy contradictions of this life; they will be of weak fiber in the awesome turmoil of *doubt*.

If I measure the greatness of God by the deeds of men in this world, I don't measure a very great or good God. If I measure the greatness of God in the world of nature, I discover a pattern of incredible order and beauty. I may concede that indeed God is the author and master designer of all of that order and beauty. But the yardstick on God's creation falls far, far short of measuring the greatness and the goodness (the grace) of God. For in his creation, I can see only where he has been. I do not meet the Designer, himself. It's like the skier's tracks in the snow. I can see where the skier has been, but that doesn't introduce me to the skier.

And if I measure God by my own feelings, my own convictions of God, I am on shaky ground. The instability of my moods and the inconsistency of my experiences make my feelings a poor means to measure the grace of God.

Then how can I be sure of God? What's he like, and how do I meet him? And was it really God the Holy Spirit that invaded my soul? Or am I operating in a grand self-delusion? Am I creating a god, or is God creating me? And is my faith of such fiber that it will see me through both life and death?"

Doubt. Uncertainty. Adrift in a stormy sea of doubt, we may well ask, as did the disciples, "Teacher, do you not care if we perish?" The wilderness of doubt, doubt about God and our relationship to him, is filled with the quicksand of despair and hopelessness.

And the great breeder of the pangs of doubt is that persistent question: "*Why?*" Why, God, did he die? Why, God, a cancer? Why, God, poverty, war, tornado, earthquake? Why, God, does love grow cold between a husband and a wife? And on and on. Choking in the dust of our "whys," we may readily smother in the broad wilderness of doubt.

But God would not have you smother in your doubt. He just may let you wander off into the wilderness, but it may be there that he can get at you with the reality of his steadfast grace. In your wilderness of doubt, God comes to assure you that God the Son, Jesus Christ, *is* the reality of God among men, that he (Christ) *is* the "Peace, be still" to the turbulent waters of your doubt.

And the truth of God's grace acting upon us is that God does *not* come to our certainties, but rather he comes to our doubts. He comes home most mightily not to our belief but to our unbelief. To respond to that call, "God, help my unbelief!" takes a God of grace, and that's the kind of a God we have!

You may have to wallow in the stormy seas of doubt to realize that, as were the disciples in that storm on Galilee. They were certain that both their boats and their skill could handle the wind and the whitecaps. What could a carpenter's son know about seamanship? But stripped of their courage, their confidence, their certainty, they woke the Master. Now Jesus did not take the tiller and guide them to safety. Rather he rebuked the wind, and said to the sea, "Peace, be still!" He rebuked the disciples also. "Have you no faith?" he asked. But in his rebuke of both the wind and the disciples, he led them to ask the right question: "Who is this? Who is this Jesus?"

And that is the question that leads us out of the wilderness of doubt. "Who is this Jesus Christ?" That is the question that directs us to God himself and to the nature of his grace. As the Spirit of God turns us to this Christ of God, we meet God himself, and we encounter a God far greater than the deeds of men in this world, far more stable than our own experience of God, a God far greater than our own ability to comprehend him.

As the Spirit of God leads us to the question: "Who is this Jesus?", the Christ himself leads us out of the wilderness of doubt. For he came into the affairs of men as God the Son, to bear a cross of grace, to die that men may live, *with God*. In Christ the fulness of God was pleased to dwell. In Christ I see God. To speak the name of Jesus Christ is to speak the name of God. Christ is indeed the reality of God among men — eternally.

As this Christ of the cross touches our hearts in the gentle urging of the Holy Spirit, the first effect is *not necessarily* one of joy and confidence. His first impact upon us is to shake us up a bit. He shatters our confidence in *ourselves* and our *certainties*. He creates doubt about the things and ideas of this world that are so sure for me. Christ comes not to my little certainties; but rather to my doubts he comes. And he comes to weave in my soul a new certainty, a new hope, a new trust. On the rubble of my shattered certainties, God builds faith. And that faith is not centered in my own good deeds, my own experience of God, or my own comprehension of God. Rather that faith is centered on that one Son of God, Jesus Christ, risen from the dead. The central certainty of my soul is God — God in Christ made real and personal in the Holy Spirit. I believe; I *trust* this Christ.

And faith *in Christ*, not faith in the quantity or purity of my faith, will see me through. The "whys" will always appear. Doubt may cast shadows into our hearts, but *nothing* — "whys" or doubts — can alter what God has done for us in this Christ of the cross and this cross of Christ. And Christian faith is engrossed with the reality of God's gracious, crucial, creative action in this Christ of the cross. Indeed faith in Christ *is* Christian certainty.

Yes, your faith in Christ is a strange and marvelous thing. From beginning to end, your faith is a miracle wrought by the creative grace of God, and every day

that faith lives on the edge of the unbe-
lievable.

And you will have doubts, times of
wonder and "why." But as God's drawing
grace keeps you in the orbit of Christ and
his cross, *you can be sure.* You can be more
sure of His certain grace than your moody
doubts; more sure of His forgiveness than
your sin; more sure of His presence than
your lostness.

As you turn in faith to Christ, he
sounds the "Peace, be still" to your
doubts, and you are at home with God, at
home from the wars in the wilderness of
doubt.

Now Moses was keeping the flock of his father-in-law, Jethro, the priest of Midian; and he led his flock to the west side of the wilderness, and came to Horeb, the mountain of God. And the angel of the Lord appeared to him in a flame of fire out of the midst of a bush; and he looked, and lo, the bush was burning, yet it was not consumed. And Moses said, "I will turn aside and see this great sight, why the bush is not burnt." When the Lord saw that he turned aside to see, God called to him out of the bush, "Moses, Moses!" And he said, "Here am I." Then he said, "Do not come near; put off your shoes from your feet, for the place on which you are standing is holy ground." And he said, "I am the God of your father, the God of Abraham, the God of Isaac, and the God of Jacob." And Moses hid his face, for he was afraid to look at God. Then the Lord said, "I have seen the affliction of my people who are in Egypt, and have heard their cry because of their taskmasters; I know their sufferings, and I have come down to deliver them out of the hand of the Egyptians, and to bring them up out of that land to a good and broad land, a land flowing with milk and honey, to the place of the Canaanites, the Hittites, the Amorites, the Perizzites, the Hivites, and the Jebusites. And now, behold, the cry of the people of Israel has come to me, and I have seen the oppression with which the Egyptians oppress them.

Come, I will send you to Pharaoh that you may bring forth my people, the sons of Israel, out of Egypt." But Moses said to God, "Who am I that I should go to Pharaoh, and bring the sons of Israel out of Egypt?" He said, "But I will be with you; and this shall be the sign for you, that I have sent you: when you have brought forth the people out of Egypt, you shall serve God upon this mountain."

Exodus 3:1–12

Grace

In

The Wilderness:

of Uncertainty

To be uncertain as to how you mesh with God's work in this world is a worrisome wilderness. Never to hear God's cordial invitation to share in the task of gathering a Kingdom, is a tragic silence. To miss out on the noble task of working alongside God breeds a deadly monotony in your daily living.

And in this wilderness silence you may well ask: "God, am I not fit for your service? Am I not good enough to make your team? Where do I belong in your grand scheme?"

The place where you work, the classroom where you study, the kitchen where you cook, may seem an unfit place for God to work the wonders of his grace. Is not the scope of God's work far too majestic for my little routine? Could God become that small as to want to work with me in my little corner of this planet?

The moment that we consider that we have no place in God's work or that he has no place in ours, we are at that time adrift in a wilderness of uncertainty. At that moment our daily living founders in a sea of monotony. With our sails furled, we no longer are driven by the winds of his grace, and we simply drift in a harsh routine. No purpose. No direction. No destination. No grace.

But perhaps the greatness of God's grace lies in the smallness of its target. He works the grand tasks of an eternal Kingdom through quite ordinary people, in quite ordinary places, as Moses discovered.

Perhaps Moses thought that he had been overlooked in God's eyes. From the Pharaoh's palace to the rocky wilderness of the Sinai desert must have seemed a step backward for Moses. No doubt he wondered: "Surely the major league problems of God cannot be worked in the minor leagues of Midian. And tending sheep seems a poor way to qualify for God's work."

But in the wilderness, God met his man. In that strange burning bush, afire but unconsumed, God led Moses out of his wilderness of uncertainty. "I am your God," he said to Moses. "I have a task for you to do, and I will be with you as you work at that task." From that moment on, Moses had purpose, direction and destination in his life. He would lead the people of God, the descendants of Abraham, Isaac and Jacob, out of the bondage of Egypt to the Promised Land.

But it wasn't quite that easy for God. Moses was reluctant about the whole business; the uncertainty in Moses ran deep. "Who am I that I should go to Pharaoh. . .?" he asked. And again, "Oh, my Lord, I am not eloquent. . . I am slow of speech and of tongue." Once more he said, "Oh, my Lord, send, I pray, some other person." Moses was gripped with uncertainty.

But God was not. He told Moses that his brother Aaron would speak for him. "Now get on with the job," God said. And Moses and Aaron went, and they led a nation (Israel) out of bondage.

Your uncertainty about both your task and your ability may also run quite deep. And yet deep in your heart you long to be involved with God and his harvest. And the tension of "I'm not up to it" pulling against the "God, I want to" puts you squarely in a wilderness of uncertainty.

And your way out of this wilderness begins, as with Moses, in your encounter with God. Worship comes always before service. Now God will not likely meet you in a burning bush. He could, of course, and we ought not place any restrictions on how he will arrange his rendezvous with us.

Nor need we wait around and continue our wandering in the wilderness. Surely we can meet our God where *we know* he may be found. And that place of certain rendezvous with God is in the Bible and in the church, whose message and power is rooted in that Book. In the words of that strange Book, I meet my God. The same Spirit of God, who inspired the men who wrote those pages, touches my reading, pondering soul, and I am eased into the orbit of God's wondrous grace. As I ponder those pages, I am held by the certainty that I *do* count with God, that I *am* fit for his service, that he *can* use me — even me.

And from those words of Scripture and in the persistent message of the church, this Man from Nazareth stands before me, *burning unconsumed*. In this eternal Son of God, I meet squarely my God. And the impact of his cross at Calvary is to disclose a God of incredible grace. For there on that cross, in the death of Christ, God the Father was enabled to treat us drifting sinners as sons. Indeed, the cross did as much for the Father as it did for us. It permitted a God of grace to mix with my fraud, my ungrace.

And that cross still burns unconsumed across our times, and the risen Christ, raised from the dead, still shines unconsumed into the darkness of our wilderness. In that eternal light you meet your God, and the exit to your wilderness of uncertainty is clear.

For he calls you to the high task of gathering a Kingdom, to labor in the harvest. And your call to his task is sounded, not so much in terms of a specific vocation, but rather it's sounded in that cross. As I ponder that cross, I am overwhelmed by the *allness* of his grace; I am convinced of the incredible *equality of his grace*. Calvary was the unleashing of his grace to all men, the great outpouring of his love into the wilderness wanderings of every man. What is sure and certain for me — his grace, his love, his cross of forgiveness — belongs with equal certainty to all men.

And there is the clue to my task. I am sent, by God, to be the carrier of his love. As he uses bread and wine and burning bushes, I am used by him as a channel for his grace. I put in his hands whatever resources I've been given, and I entrust to him what I lack, and I move out with him to meet my neighbor. In that world of other people lies the great frontier of faith, and certain that God is with us, faith becomes a grand venture of grace-in-action.

You may not lead a nation out of captivity, as did Moses. Your life with God may not seem spectacular. But sensitive to the wondrous grace of your God and sensitive to the needs of your brother, every common task takes on a Godly dimension. Your office, your classroom, and your kitchen are places where the burning grace of God can burn unconsumed, and as you rendezvous with God *there*, in the place that you are, your life takes on purpose and direction. And the wilderness of uncertainty is flooded with the wondrous grace of God.

Now when Job's three friends heard of all this evil that had come upon him, they came each from his own place. Eliphaz the Temanite, Bildad the Shuhite, and Zophar the Naamathite. They made an appointment together to come to condole with him and comfort him. And when they saw him from afar, they did not recognize him; and they raised their voices and wept; and they rent their robes and sprinkled dust upon their heads toward heaven. And they sat with him on the ground seven days and seven nights, and no one spoke a word to him, for they saw that his suffering was very great.

Job 2:11–13

Then Job answered the Lord: "I know that thou canst do all things, and that no purpose of thine can be thwarted. 'Who is this that hides counsel without knowledge?' Therefore I have uttered what I did not understand, things too wonderful for me, which I did not know. . ."

Job 42:1–3

Grace

In

The Wilderness:

of Suffering

Our suffering, in whatever form it takes, can back us into a barren wasteland of torment. For it reminds us that we are human, that we are fragile, and that we are destructible. And we don't like that.

And no one escapes this wilderness. At the moment of our birth, the doctor lifts us by the ankles and swats us right on the bottom, and we cry. Now this maneuver clears the lungs, but the sting is in our back side. Early in life we experience pain, and we weave in and out of the wilderness of this distress throughout our days.

In countless ways people hurt. Sickness, accidents, battle wounds, and cancers cause immeasureable physical pain. The dimensions of human suffering exceed our human comprehension. And perhaps the physical discomfort is the easiest to tolerate. We may steel ourselves to its pangs, and in time we may even adjust to its presence. But the mental, the emotional, and the spiritual sufferings are perhaps the less easy to tolerate. In the wilderness of mental, emotional, and moral confusion, we wander a barren wasteland of fear, loneliness and prejudice. Indeed, our suffering, in whatever form it takes — physical, emotional, spiritual — can become an awesome wilderness of despair.

And the Christian is not exempt. He may suffer great pain in his lifetime. Sensitive to the affliction of his brother, the Christian may suffer intensely from his brother's distress. Christians know the whole spectrum of human suffering — broken legs and broken hearts, shattered limbs and shattered dreams, gnawing cancer and gnawing guilt. Your exposure to God is no certain waiver from suffering.

To the Christian, the reality of human suffering unleashes a flurry or questions. "If you're so good, God, why must I suffer so much? If you're so powerful, God, heal me! Must I suffer my way into heaven? God, I believe — now lift this awesome pall of pain." Indeed, the wilderness of suffering is a bleak, spiritual desert, too, and a man's relationship with God can deteriorate rapidly as the pangs of suffering spread their seeds of despair.

And the problem with suffering is that it's such a personal, self-contained, thing. I cannot really share your pain, nor can I give up a portion of my discomfort to you. At the bedside of a suffering son, or daughter, or parent, I may wish mightily that I could take unto myself the burden of their pain. But that I cannot do. I can commit my suffering, and theirs, to the latest medical techniques, and relief is usually swift and comforting. For these gifts of medicine I am grateful, but they only suppress the suffering; they do not remove it. They may soothe, but they do not heal.

When close to one who is suffering, we find little to say. At the side of a suffering friend, we are essentially speechless in the face of his torment. The friends of Job were silent for a while: "No one spoke a word to him, for they saw that his suffering was very great." Words that comfort are elusive, for the depths of human misery are far too great for human pity or human sympathy. In bearing the pain of another, the empathy of the human heart can go only so far — no further.

And in the face of a man's struggle with his God over the matter of his suffering, no quick and shallow answers will do. After an initial silence, the friends of Job spoke. In numerous and eloquent words, they showered Job with advice, but their advice only deepened Job's anger. In the wilderness of his suffering, Job needed more than words of comfort, more than words of condolence. He needed his God; he needed the assurance of the power of God working in the midst of his suffering. For forty chapters the book of Job unfolds the anguish of Job's struggle with both his counselors and his God. Job suffered; Job struggled — *but finally Job surrendered.* Convinced of God's great power and his own humanness, Job yielded his suffering, his pride, his life to the creative hands of God. "I know that thou canst do all things, and that no purpose of thine can be thwarted."

Now surely God prefers that we not suffer. It is not God's will that we suffer and hurt. It is no comfort at all to say, "It's God's will that you suffer." Surely, the Father has no desire to see his many sons suffer. Surely, God would much prefer that we be fit for his service, in both physical and emotional ways.

For God knows the extent and depth of human suffering. In the form of a Savior on a cross, God tasted the loneliness and the pain of human suffering. God spared not his own Son, and there at Calvary he suffered to an extent *far greater* than we will ever know. There the sinless Christ bore the entire burden of human sin. He bore it to God, that God could forgive.

The Christ of the cross did not suffer that we may not. Rather he suffered on the cross that God may come to us and that we may draw close to him. "Through him (Christ) we have obtained access to this grace in which we stand. . . (Rom. 5:2). In the hands of God, Christ's suffering was turned to victory — victory for God, and victory for us. There lies the clue to this matter of our own suffering. *We put it squarely in the hands of God, that through our cross of suffering, he may draw ever closer to us.* Through suffering, God found

Job, and Job discovered a closeness to God that he had never known before. ". . .things too wonderful for me, which I did not know," said Job.

So with us. In the face of suffering, we are *not* speechless. There *are* words to say, words of power and strength. In the wilderness of suffering, we can pray mightily that the suffering be lifted from us, that the healing hand of God may ease the pain and restore the health.

But is there not a greater prayer than that? Is it not a higher thing to pray that suffering be used by God for his coming than for pain's removal? Surely we pray for the lifting of our suffering, but the greater hope lies in pain's conversion rather than in its removal. As God uses bread and wine as a means of his grace, the greater prayer is that God may use our suffering as a bearer of his grace, his strength, his capturing love, and his powerful presence. Indeed, we pray that God would exploit our turmoil for his purpose with us, to draw near in the midst of this wilderness.

Our suffering reminds us that we are indeed human, fragile, destructible. It just might be our first introduction to the reality of death. But as this suffering drives us closer to God, as it brings God closer to us, there is a powerful blessing in it. That blessing is not the removal of our suffering, but the great blessing is the coming of God himself into our lives.

"And after you have suffered a little while, the God of all grace, who has called you to His eternal glory in Christ, will himself restore, establish and strengthen you. To him be the dominion for ever and ever. Amen." (1 Peter 5:10–11)

"He who is faithful in a very little is faithful also in much; and he who is dishonest in a very little is dishonest also in much. If then you have not been faithful in the unrighteous mammon, who will entrust to you the true riches? And if you have not been faithful in that which is another's, who will give you that which is your own? No servant can serve two masters; for either he will hate the one and love the other, or he will be devoted to the one and despise the other. You cannot serve God and mammon."

Luke 16:10–13

Grace

In

The Wilderness:

of Conflict

Every man's soul is a battleground. For there the powerful forces of good and evil wage a violent conflict. "For I do not do the good I want, but the evil I do not want is what I do" belongs to each one of us as it did to the Apostle Paul. The tension of "God, to Thee belongs the glory" versus "Can't I keep a little for myself" puts us squarely in a wilderness of conflict. In the face of our persistent withholding from God, He confronts us with those haunting words, "No servant can serve two masters." At the moment we enter the service of two masters, we enter a barren wilderness of conflict. For inevitably we will love one and hate the other.

And hate and love shape an intense conflict. And no Christian can avoid the wilderness.

Now, one solution to the easing of this tension is to reject completely God's claim upon us. "I will take the controls of this ship — I will be the ship's Master." This was the course that Adam took at Eden. "I will determine the fruits of the garden that I shall eat, and I will be like God, knowing good and evil." In a stange way, God permits this mutiny. He has created us free to reject both his claim upon us and his grace for us.

But this apparent freedom is no freedom at all. It may appear as an attractive exit from the wilderness of conflict that permeates our soul, but it only shackles us with a bondage to which *there is no exit*. To deliberately invalidate God's claim upon you leads only to potholes of quicksand in the wilderness, a quicksand in which we smother in self-serving, self-righteousness, self-smallness. We literally die without the oxygen of his grace. To reject God is no solution to our conflict; it leads only to death in the wilderness.

If that is no solution to the tension within us, what then is? How can I live with this clash of wills — *His* versus *mine*? How can I wander this wilderness and avoid the potholes?

Well, our exit lies with God and with the nature of his claim upon us. How much does God ask for? And can I not withhold a fair share for myself? When you ponder the nature of God's claim upon you in the light of the cross and the Resurrection of the Son of God, you become increasingly aware that God's claim upon you is *total, authentic,* and *complete.* The Christ died that we may live as sons, that we may live *today* free of this bondage of mutiny. In the Christ of the cross and the Lord of the Empty Tomb, God withheld nothing from you. In this strong Son of God, you have been given, *by grace, all* that you need for a full, free life with God. Perhaps not all you *want*, but in the grace of the cross, you've been given all that you need.

And there at the foot of the cross, you are aware that God's claim is total — *all* that you are, *all* that you have. *The total loyalty of the soul* — that's what God asks for. He will settle for nothing less: "I am the Lord your God; you shall have no other gods before me." There on the cross, there in the Risen Christ, the issue of his Lordship was settled, *one* for *all*, and as God gains that same victory in the conflict of your soul, you yield to the one Master. The completeness of his grace establishes the totality of his claim.

But you may not like that. It just may be too much for you. What about my "fair share?" Have I no "rights" before God? If I could sidestep the cross, if I might somehow blot out the cross at Calvary, then perhaps I could build a bargaining position before God. I could appeal to him on the basis of the law — the Ten Commandments. After all, I'm told, one cannot really keep the whole Law, but still I may point out that I do the best I can. And I might argue that generally I do pretty well. I live by the Golden Rule. I live and let live. Or I might build my case on some form of a "godly curve." "I know I'm not perfect, God, but look at all these lousy people around me. Am I not a cut above them?" On and on I can fabricate a babble of self-serving excuses before God.

But the awful silence of the cross shatters my glib charade. As I turn to the cross and consider carefully the Savior dying there, I am speechless before my God. The grace of that cross silences before it saves, and the most that any man can say is, "Lord, have mercy upon us." The grace of that cross bursts the bubble of my self-righteousness, and drives me to the reality that I have no "inalienable" rights before God. I cannot bargain with him, for he has not bartered with me. The grace of God in Jesus Christ is enough to humble a man.

And *there*, in what I would call a humility relationship with God, through faith in Jesus Christ, lies our hope in this wilderness of conflict. "But he gives more grace; therefore it says, 'God opposes the proud, but gives grace to the humble.'" (James 4:6)

This humility before God grows out of the clear recognition that we have no bargaining rights before him. Our humility relationship with God is not something we have in the sight of other people. It is not a matter of servility, lowliness, or meekness in our relationships with one another. It may take the form of modesty before men, or it may not. And it can take an active, fiery shape in the face of injustice and prejudice. It has to do with how we stand before God, not how we appear in the eyes of others.

And this humility before God is possible only to faith. It rests squarely on our deep sense of what God has done for us in the Christ of the cross, on a deep sense of God's wondrous love, on a deep sense of our mutiny *as mastered by God's grace.* Humility is the heart's attitude to God, the total loyalty of the soul to God and to God alone.

> Nothing in my hand I bring,
> Simply to Thy Cross I cling;
> Naked, come to Thee for dress;
> Helpless, look to Thee for grace. . .

Captured by his grace, you trust God, and you serve the One you trust. Yet the conflict within your heart continues. This is one wilderness that you cannot avoid or completely escape. But as the battle rages in your soul, you fix your eyes upon the Commander; you trust your God; you commit your cause to him, and the wilderness of conflict is eased as God commands your first loyalty. Captured and held by this grace you serve God, not mammon.

Now there was a man of the Pharisees, named Nicodemus, a ruler of the Jews. This man came to Jesus by night and said to him, "Rabbi, we know that you are a teacher come from God; for no one can do these signs that you do, unless God is with him." Jesus answered him, "Truly, truly, I say to you, unless one is born anew, he cannot see the kingdom of God." Nicodemus said to him, "How can a man be born when he is old? Can he enter a second time into his mother's womb and be born?" Jesus answered, "Truly, truly, I say to you, unless one is born of water and the Spirit, he cannot enter the kingdom of God. That which is born of the flesh is flesh, and that which is born of the Spirit is spirit. Do not marvel that I said to you, 'You must be born anew.' The wind blows where it wills, and you hear the sound of it, but you do not know whence it comes or whither it goes; so it is with every one who is born of the Spirit." Nicodemus said to him, "How can this be?"

John 3:1–9

Grace

In

The Wilderness:

of Rationalism

The grace of God does not always make "sense." Nor does God appeal to our "common sense." The moment that we insist that God fit neatly into our rational thought patterns, *we lose Him.* Our demand for a rational, provable God backs us into a wilderness where God has extreme difficulty in reaching us. As we apply our deductive reasoning to the ways of God, we drift in a wilderness of confusion.

The voice of science offers us no exit from this wilderness. Long years ago Francis Bacon (1561–1626) said that knowledge is power, and generations since have pressed hard this pursuit of knowledge. With a passion to know, men have probed deeply into the mysteries of this planet. And we in this generation have been witnesses to an astounding accumulation of knowledge. "Data banks" are required to store it all.

Surely much, much good comes from this press for knowledge. The richness that the scientist has added to our lives is immeasurable. The years that I spent in the scientific and engineering community were rich, fascinating years. I am grateful for those years.

But to the central issues of life and death, the methods of science offer little input. The voice of the systematic, rational approach grows quiet as a man seeks to know God, as a man seeks to be known by God. You simply cannot apply the techniques of "systems engineering" to his grace; you cannot "prove" God in a laboratory or a surgery room.

And this makes us uneasy. We are conditioned to this kind of approach. In all our decision making, we try to apply a reasonable process. We gather the facts; we analyze the data; we examine the alternatives; then we make a decision. Now, it's not all that clear-cut. Our feelings, our personal preferences, our "hunches," our whole personality, cloud the purity of our scientific approach, and we make bad choices. But we strive for the "sensible" approach in our daily living, and we expect people to "make sense" to us.

And we expect God to "make sense" also. We want Him on our terms, in our neat, rational thought categories. Insisting that he reveal himself to us in clear-cut, logical sequences, we miss our God and his majestic grace; we wander a barren desert of rationalism.

No, God doesn't reach out to our common sense. Rather *he touches our personality — all that we are, the soul — and not our rationality alone.* He invades the human heart, not simply the thinking chambers of the mind. He seeks our loyalty, our trust, our faith, and these responses do not arise from a soul conditioned only by logic. Indeed, God's ways are not our ways.

Nicodemus discovered this.

"How can this be?" he asked. As Jesus unfolded the mystery of seeing and entering the Kingdom of God, Nicodemus could only ask, "How can this be? How can a man be born when he is old?" It was a rational response to the mystery of conversion. For Nicodemus, the winds of grace were a fit subject for meterology, not for God's encounter with a man. The radical nature of rebirth by grace, *through faith,* didn't make sense to Nicodemus, and he missed his God who stood right before him in the person of Jesus Christ.

Indeed your commitment to God, through faith in Jesus Christ, is a strange thing. You believe in a Father, a Christ, a Spirit that you have never seen, or touched, or heard (at least in a measurable audio frequency). Born of water and the Spirit, you thirst for God. With the Word and water, he keeps you thirsty. It doesn't really make sense.

But it didn't make sense for Abraham to walk with his son, Isaac, to the top of Mount Moriah. It didn't make sense for David to stand up to Goliath with only a slingshot. It didn't make sense for Peter and his brother to leave their fishing boats to follow Christ. It didn't make sense for Paul to travel to Rome. But bound in trust to God, they worked the tasks of an eternal Kingdom. They did not wait for a systematic analysis of the facts, but rather in faith they followed their God.

It is not natural (reasonable) for a man to believe in God. Our inherent nature is to want no part of him, and we are disturbed that the dimensions of God far exceed our rational comprehension. That's why this rebirth from this life to an eternal life is such a radical maneuver. It takes a new creation, a new loyalty of the heart, and a new response to the Father's creative hand. And like Peter we need to be converted over and over and over again.

The new life with God requires the creative grace of God. *That's precisely why Christ came.* He came not to answer the question, "How can this be?" but rather to say, "It is finished! He who believes in me, though he die, yet shall he live." In a strange way God is hidden to our rational comprehension of him. He doesn't really "prove" himself to us by arriving with overwhelming credentials. The birth of Jesus, the death of Christ, and the Resurrection of our Lord do not "prove" God to us. Rather the cross of Christ and the Easter resurrection convey the creative grace of God, and that creative grace is our one source of new life, new birth. As that eternal act of God on the cross comes home to each one of us, riding on the winds of the Holy Spirit, our response is not "How can this be?" but rather *"God, I believe."* The Christ of the cross is as creative today as he was at Calvary, as he was "in the beginning." *Faith* — that's our response to God's grace. The grace of God, born on the Gospel of Jesus Christ, creates in us the power to believe.

So "by faith we understand" (Heb. 11:3). In faith, Abraham, David, Peter, and Paul understood. *Faith* — that's our one great debt to God; that's our grand response to his grace that acts in love to one another. *Faith* — that's our grand trust in God that passes far beyond our rational comprehension. Faith is the grand venture in which we commit our whole present and our whole future to the certainty that Christ is the reality of God, that in him our sins are forgiven, that in the same heavenly Father my neighbor is my brother.

It may not make sense. The Christian faith is filled with the irrational. Now, that is not to say that Christians are irrational; they are as rational or irrational as anybody else. But Christian faith lives on the edge of the unprovable and is wrapped in a web of mystery.

So as you ponder the grand dimensions of his grace, *let the mystery remain.* Let the unknowns of his infinite grace haunt you, captivate you, and hold you for an eternal Kingdom. Your faith, created by God himself, is your one exit from the wilderness of rationalism.

Indeed not everything makes sense — the beauty of a rose, the warm spell of a fireplace, the sweet mystery of grace. God is not the only reality we cannot "prove."

We seek not proof; we open our hearts to his grace, and *believing, we receive it.*

"Therefore I tell you, do not be anxious about your life, what you shall eat or what you shall drink, nor about your body, what you shall put on. Is not life more than food, and the body more than clothing?"

Matthew 6:25

Grace

In

The Wilderness:

of Worry

Is not life more than food and clothing, a steady job — better yet, an interesting, self-fulfilling job — a nice home, and Social Security in old age? Most will agree that life *is* more than these, and that there is a dimension of life that spills beyond the necessities and routines of daily existing.

But all will agree that these are very important. The realities of living out each day dictate the need for food, clothing and shelter. And what about tomorrow, those distant years of old age? Will there be security beyond the productive years? Indeed, the needs and the frailty of the body make harsh demands upon us.

And we worry. Caught in the tensions produced by our human physical needs on one hand and our uncertainty as to our ability to meet them on the other, we worry. We are anxious. And perhaps a bit afraid. Where will it all come from? What about tomorrow?

In this wilderness of worry, life is robbed of its joy, its peace, and its purpose. Corroded by worry, our spirits drag, and we stagnate in weariness. As with the witches in Shakespeare's *Macbeth,* it's all: "Double, double toil and trouble; Fire burn and cauldron bubble." Indeed, the fire of worry burns brightly in the cauldrons of our uncertainties; it smolders in the contradictions and the desperations of everyday living.

Is there no escape from this barren wilderness? Is not life more than just scrambling to make ends meet? No more than just an unholy deadlock between what I have and what I think I ought to have?

From this wilderness of worry, attractive exits beckon. "Try me," they say. "I will offer you a security that will cleanse your heart of its anxiety."

One of these beguiling exits is to *give up,* to seek avenues of dependence. If I cannot provide for my physical needs, I will seek those persons or institutions who can. I will become as a child, and seek that mother or father who took such good care of me. I will give up my manhood and my integrity for a security blanket of paternalism. Yet still I worry. I worry mightily that the fountain that supplies my needs may dry up. I may worry less about my needs, but more about the reliability of the giver. Through this exit of giving up, I move from one wilderness to another.

Or you may seek another exit from your anxiety. You may choose to "pile it up," to accumulate such a large portion of the world's wealth that surely it will last "forever." And you will build bigger and better barns in which to store it and to hoard it. You may have to sacrifice your integrity here also, for do not the worthy ends of security justify the means? Yet here, too, in the midst of plenty, you are uneasy. You fret. Will the barns burn down? In this fast changing world, will the goods in the barn today meet the needs of tomorrow? And your conscience keeps the cauldron burning as you see the haunting needs of your brother. The barns of plenty don't really soothe the pangs of worry. In a strange way, the barns of plenty lead us into a deeper, more persistent anxiety. For they open the dimensions of *guilt*, and this only darkens the wilderness of worry.

Now most of us roam the wilderness between these apparent exits of absolute dependence and absolute independence. Perhaps these are the extremes that we choose not to follow. Instead we may choose to remain in this wilderness, and somehow steel ourselves to its corrosive influence. We will "grin and bear it," or ignore our worry in the wishful thinking that "somehow" the cause of our fears will go away. Or we may let our worry become a matter of pride, a little god that feeds our self-righteousness. "We love because we worry" becomes a little religion of self-justification.

Is there no other exit to this wilderness of worry than these — giving up, hoarding it, or living with it?

Well, there is, and it lies squarely with God. Worry needs God, or it becomes a god.

You may respond to that by saying, "Come on, pastor, it's not all that simple. I've tried God; yet still I worry." Well, perhaps that's it. You've put God on trial, *rather than trust Him.* You program Him to your needs and await the results. If His response is not immediate or to your liking, you give up on Him. And you worry.

"Whom do you *trust?* And what do you

trust?" These are extremely important questions for every man, for they lead clearly to a dimension of life that far exceeds our obsession with security. "Is not life more than food. . .?" is the haunting question that leads to the greater question: "Whom do you trust?"

As you trust God, your anxiety is eased, not by the perfection and purity of your trust, but because God is the one *trustworthy reality of this world.* Indeed, your faith in God is a trust in God before it is anything else. To say, "I believe" is to say, "I trust."

This trust in God grows (it may take some time) out of our certain realization that everything we have, everything we are, and everything we will have is given to us by God. We have *nothing* we have not received. We belong to God, and he has never annuled his claim upon us. The certainty of his eternal care has been confirmed to us in an eternal act of grace — the ageless act of the cross. The Christ who died there said, "Father, forgive them. . ." *"Father"* — that was his one-ness with God; *"forgive them"* — that was his great act of grace.

There lies your trust. You trust this strong Son of God. Deep down in your soul you lean on him; you are certain that he is very, very close; sure of his steadfast grace, *you are confident.* This trust of Christ, the Son of God, is the highest commit-ment a man can make. The compelling bond that God weaves in your heart by His wondrous grace puts certainty and confidence in your soul. You trust God more than yourself; you trust God's trust in you more than your ability to under-stand it. You join with the Psalmist in declaring:

> But I trust in thee, O Lord,
>   I say, "Thou are my God."
> My times are in thy hand.

Psalm 31:14–16

Our times are in God's hands — our past, our present, our future — and we rest in the certainty that God is God, and we are the precious sheep of his pasture. We trust our God, and back through our trust comes the gift of eternal life and ultimate security. It takes courage to trust God, but your trust in God feeds on his grace in Christ Jesus and then generates its own courage. And what is it about God that you trust? You trust his steadfast grace in Jesus Christ.

In this solid relationship of trust, you cast your anxieties on God, and you are eased out of this wilderness of worry.

Out of the depths I cry to thee,
*   O Lord!*
Lord, hear my voice!
Let thy ears be attentive
*   to the voice of my supplica-*
*   tions!*
If thou, O Lord, shouldst mark in-
*   iquities,*
*   Lord, who could stand?*
But there is forgiveness with thee,
*   that thou mayest be feared.*

Psalm 130:1–4

Then those who were at table with him began to say
among themselves, "Who is this, who even forgives
sins?"

Luke 7:49

Grace

In

The Wilderness:

of Guilt

Guilt poisons the wells of the soul. It's a grinding burden that prevents a man from reaching the soaring heights of purity and cleanness that his heart longs for. Like ice on the wings of an airplane, guilt drags a man down from the performance that was designed into him. Like friction in the bearings of a motor, it consumes the energy of the soul. It reminds us that we are men and not angels. It drives us to hide from ourselves, from each other, and from God.

Indeed the wilderness of guilt is a lifelong search for secluded hide-outs. *For who wants to face a judge when he knows that he is guilty?* Guilt implies a judge, and the guilty man knows it. Faced with the certainty that he must stand before a judge, a man has two alternatives: he can seek to hide the evidence, or he can seek to avoid the judge. Either course drives a man deeper and deeper into the wilderness as he seeks mightily to cover over the evidence, to become lost from the judge.

But the poison wells of the wilderness offer little comfort. I may achieve some success in burying my guilt from myself. After all, I'm not an angel, and my humanity appeals to itself with a babble of excuses. And I might achieve considerable success in masking off my guilt from the judgment of others. I will wear a perennial smile. Surely, a happy face will conceal the internal turmoil of shame. I may look a bit silly doing that, but I will take that risk rather than expose my haunting guilt to the judgment of others.

But before God — *no place, no way to hide!* Neither my excuses nor my smiles can cover over my consistent shortcomings before him. I'm wide-open before God, and I rebel mightily at this exposure. The haunting words of God the Son press close: "You are those who justify yourselves before men, but God knows your hearts."(Luke 16:15) *He knows my heart!* And that's too much. To him I plead, "Search my mind, consider my thoughts, look through my inventory of good works, weigh my fine intentions, but God, stay out of the inner chambers of my soul!" For there lies the sin that I know is there, that I long to hide. This sin — this willful departure from God, this deliberate mutiny against his authority, this deliberate rejection of his claim upon his sons — turns my Eden into a wilderness of guilt. This sin corrodes the fibers of the soul, and keeps me alone in a barren and bleak desert. I cannot hide the guilt; I cannot avoid the Judge.

Yet still we try. We yield to our Judge reluctantly. We avoid facing him squarely.

We may try an appeal to the Judge on the basis of the law-keeping the Ten Commandments, living by the Golden Rule, being "very good." After all, God himself gave us the Ten Commandments. Surely, He will consider this approach favorably. As we pursue this course with pious intent, we slowly become aware of our fraud. For we discover that our motives are not pure, that we glorify only ourselves, that we use the laws of God at our convenience, that we are not always very "good." But in our attempts at keeping the law, we gradually become more sensitive to the Law-Giver as we note our dismal performance before him. The law eventually condemns, and guilt increases.

Or we may appeal to our consciences in a grand display of self-justification. We will let our consciences be our guide, and "I" will be the judge. But the burning conscience will not maintain order in the court of the soul. It probes; it needles; it persistently reminds us, "You're not measuring up." Powerless to forgive, the conscience haunts us with our guilt. Like the law, the conscience can only condemn.

With no place to hide, no way to avoid the Judge, we come squarely against the question: "If thou, O Lord, shouldst mark iniquities, Lord who could stand?" And in the wilderness of our guilt, we arrive at the awesome truth: *no one. Not one!*

Is there no exit from this wilderness? How can any man be right with God? How can I cool this simmering conscience?

And God's answer to these questions is a message of grace: *"Your sins are forgiven!"*

In a strange way the exit from this wilderness of sin and guilt is not of our doing. It rests with God himself, and squarely with God our restless hearts find their rest from this awesome wilderness.

For God did not create us free to sin

without keeping to himself a greater power to save. All the energy of God was not expended in those six days of creation. His great power was held in reserve to seek us in the wilderness of guilt, sin and death — to seek us and to save us for himself. He wants us in the Father's fold. He would not leave us in the wilderness of separation.

And it took a Savior, a cross, and a tomb, empty of death, to atone for our guilt, our sin. In this Jesus of Nazareth, God made the decisive move to keep us for himself. We deserve death, we are guilty, and it was death he gave us — *but it was the death of a Savior*. In the cross of Christ and the resurrection of our Lord sin, death, guilt — our violence to God and his ways — were swallowed up in a victory of grace. In the cross of Christ, the guilt of all men collided violently with the grace of God. The Son of God did not come to *explain* our sin, or to *speculate* upon it. He came not even to condemn it. But rather he came to *effect* forgiveness, to open the way for God to come to his wandering sons, to make us right with God himself. God's great object with us is to commune with us in a living, dynamic, daily, holy communion, and the cross and the resurrection makes this communion rendezvous possible. There is no communion between us and God without the forgiveness of our sins. But that's been done! The cross *is* God's judgment on the world. By the Christ who died there, our sins are forgiven. It is done. The Judge is on our side.

But it is not the *fact* of Christ's death and resurrection that saves you from your wilderness of guilt. Rather it's the inner nature of that fact as understood by your personal faith. Your forgiveness before God, anchored in the cross of years ago, becomes real and certain for you as it is anchored in your soul by the time-spanning, individualizing action of the Holy Spirit. As the Spirit of God opens your heart to the certainty that Christ bled and died *for you,* that in him, *your* sins are forgiven, you experience a strange peace, a pure water for your thirsty soul. Your restless heart rests in the assurance that you're all right with God, that he will have you, guilt and all.

"Who is this that even forgives sins?" It's Christ the Lord, the Son of God, and His authority rests squarely on a cross and an empty tomb. As the same risen Savior finds us in our wilderness of guilt, we hear those words of eternal grace: "Your sins are forgiven. Come back home to your gracious Father where you belong."

And in faith, in trust, we come. Out of the wilderness we come, found by grace, forgiven by grace, alive in grace.

Working together with him, then, we entreat you not to accept the grace of God in vain. For he says,
"At the acceptable time I have listened
to you,
and helped you on the day of salvation."
Behold, now is the acceptable time; behold now is the day of salvation.

2 Corinthians 6:1–2

And this is eternal life, that they know thee the only true God, and Jesus Christ whom thou hast sent.

John 17:3

Grace

In

The Wilderness:

of Procrastination

Tomorrow just won't do. Mañana is not the acceptable time. At least not for God. He wants you now — *today.* For if he can't reach you today, the likelihood is slim that he can reach you tomorrow. In a strange way, time can harden the human heart to God's coming.

Time is a fickle lover. In our youth, she seduces us into thinking that we have an infinite supply. In mid-life, she makes hints that she'll pull out. In old age, her hints of withdrawal are positively confirmed. As time passes, we view it from quite different perspectives. In our youth, we look forward; in the middle years, we are much concerned with the present; in our old age, we look back. The value of time changes as it elapses for us. In our youth we measure time from our birth; in the latter years we measure it to the end — death. Like diamonds and gold, the value of time is measured by its scarcity, not by its abundance. We can measure our time from birth, but we are not able to measure its true value. For we cannot measure the time to the "end" — to death.

And *there* is the rub; that's the wilderness. The unknowns of future duration keep us always in a wilderness of uncertainty. There may be no tomorrow.

In a strange way there may be no tomorrow for God. Oh, he will have his tomorrows; they will go on eternally. But if he can't take hold in your life today, there may be no tomorrow for you or for God. How God works beyond that horizon of death is far outside human understanding. Death is irrational and is beyond our comprehension. And we ought not speculate too much on God's ways beyond death, but rather we ought to consider seriously that we are given *this* lifetime to get to know God. And we ought to be sure that whatever delays we put before him, whatever postponement and procrastination we offer to him, only increases the likelihood that he can never know us, or we him. The deliberate postponement of faith here and now in the hope of doing it "later" only conditions the heart to its never happening. *No one, not one,* is guaranteed the last moment of faith that saved the repentant thief on that cross beside Jesus. Clearly, in terms of time, we are guaranteed nothing, and our procrastination only frustrates God as it robs us of the grand dimensions that God intends for our lives, as it robs us of the certainties that God can put into our hearts. The wilderness of procrastination is a wilderness for both God and us.

Our days need not be that way. Time,

like grace, is given to us by God for a purpose. It's given to us that we may come to know God through the indestructible bond of faith in Christ, and it's given to us to expend wisely in his service.

You may draw close to God today. By the grace of God in an eternal Christ, you may come near to God. *Now,* at this moment. That is the Gospel, the startling good news that we now have access to God. "Through him we have obtained access to this grace in which we stand, and we rejoice in our hope of sharing the glory of God" (Romans 5:2). Indeed our certain hope lies in our *present* possession of this Son of God.

Where can you find your God today? Where can you make this holy rendezvous with him? Well, you certainly will miss him in your wilderness of procrastination. You can want to be found by him. Surely, he is well hidden, but Christian certainty begins with the truth that God wants to be known — known by you now, in a very personal way, on *this* side of the curtain of death. Long years ago, God broke the silence of the ages and came into our kind of time to make himself known to the hearts of men. In this God-Man from Nazareth, the full grace of God was unfolded before men. As you see Christ by faith, you see God for sure.

And you'll more likely encounter this Christ of God where he said he would be. You'll meet him today where two or three are gathered in His name. You'll meet him in the Scriptures, for they were written "that you may believe that Jesus is the Christ, the Son of God, and that believing you may have life in his name" (John 20:31). You are more likely to meet Him in those who know Him than among those who do not. It may take some time, but that's why it's been given to you.

And it's the present tense of Christ we seek, not just a firmer impression of a man from the past. As Christ lives for us *now,* then faith lives in us *now.* And this would not be possible without the Spirit of God working in our hearts and minds. As the Holy Spirit acquires us, we are eased into a gentle docking maneuver with the living Christ. The Spirit of truth makes the person of Christ near, alive, real, and intimate. The God who came into the affairs of men long ago comes to each man as Christ comes to him in the time-compressing action of the Holy Spirit. As the Spirit creates in us the power to believe, we yield to our Lord, and time begins to lose its dominion over us.

That is God's ultimate purpose in giving us the time that He has provided to us — that time may lose its dominion over us, *that we may be free of its limits*. We are given time that we may move from *clock* time to *eternal* time. *Eternal life* is God's great gift of grace to every man, woman, and child who comes under the spell of this strong Son of God.

God's view of time differs quite radically from ours. For us, it's the ticking of the clock in day-by-day increments. For us it begins, and it appears to terminate. Not so for God. To him a day is as thousand years, a thousand years as a day. For him it has no beginning and no end. So our movement from our time to his time is a strange and radical maneuver. It has nothing to do really with time's duration; it is not a matter of longevity. *Rather it has to do with our present relationship to God through believing in Jesus Christ.* Eternal life is a present, contemporary relationship with God, not a matter of everlasting time. "And this *is* eternal life, that they know thee the only true God, and Jesus Christ whom thou hast sent" (John 17:3). Don't ever lose sight of these words of our Lord. *Eternal life is faith in Jesus Christ.* It's not something we enter beyond the horizon of death; it's something that captures us on this side of the horizon. It's not a goal of the future, but rather an inner attitude toward God now. It's not something we may expect from God; rather it's an inner, personal power created by his present grace. As you come to God through faith in Christ, *you have it. Eternal life is yours.*

And this certainty, this confidence, this present inner peace, is what you miss in your delay, your postponement, your wilderness of procrastination. So tomorrow won't do either for you or for God. The time we have is a gift of grace, that he may establish his bridgehead of eternity within us. And we ought not delay in permitting him to do that — for his sake and ours. We ought not abuse that gift by putting Him off, but rather we offer time to Him that he may weave the bonds of eternity into our souls.

And right now, this day, is the acceptable time. Through faith in Christ, *today* is our day of salvation. We may not have all the calendar time that we want. But as we use our time to let God intercept us, then the Spirit of God ushers us into eternity, into life with God that knows no end. We have been given time to know God, through faith in the eternal Son.

And that's all the time that we need.

And his gifts were that some should be apostles,
some prophets, some evangelists, some pastors and
teachers, for the equipment of the saints, for the work
of ministry, for building up the body of Christ, until
we all attain to the unity of the faith and of the
knowledge of the Son of God, to mature manhood, to
the measure of the stature of the fulness of Christ; so
that we may no longer be children, tossed to and fro
and carried about with every wind of doctrine, by the
cunning of men, by their craftiness in deceitful wiles.
Rather, speaking the truth in love, we are to grow
up in every way into him who is the head, into
Christ. . .

Ephesians 4:11–15

Grace

In

The Wilderness:

of Growing Up

This matter of growing up is really not a matter of the calendar. Maturity is not necessarily a matter of years piled upon years. But rather the man of mature depth is one who has grown up "in every way into him who is the head, into Christ."

Maturity then, at least in a Christian sense, is a matter of grace — God's grace in Christ Jesus.

Certainly we measure maturity by standards other than our relationship to God. The "grownup" is one whose judgment is stable in times of crisis, whose insight into the ways of the world is such that he can discern the good from the evil. Adulthood is measured in terms of emotional stability, of broad knowledge, of moral character, of personal compassion. The mature individual is viewed as one who can adjust to changes, as one who can "handle" personal temptations, as one who is free from devotion to personal power, free from personal prejudice. The mature man is one with the depth and the courage to move through failure to new avenues of service. "I tried; I failed, but I'll try again." This is the mark of a mature man. And there are other marks of maturity. You may add your own as you see them.

Yet these characteristics of the "grownup" *may* or *may not* be the marks of the Christian. The dimensions of Christian maturity far exceed our capability of displaying them before the eyes of men. Some may possess most of the characteristics mentioned above, but in terms of God's stamp upon them they are as "children, tossed to and fro and carried about by every word of doctrine. . ."

And there is the wilderness of growing up. Without God's grip upon us, we are as children tossed about in a wilderness of "deceitful wiles." It's a wilderness quite apart from our chronological age. Some are found by the grace of God early in life, others later, some never.

Although growing pains occur at every stage of our lives, perhaps we ought to pause a moment to look at those years when growing up is such a confusing wilderness. I refer to the years of our youth — the teen years and the early adult years. These are the years when life begins to move in extremes — up all night, sleep all day. These are the years when good judgment is veiled by the emotions, where acceptance by the group dominates our individuality, when the search for freedom dulls our sense of responsibility. But those are the warm and sensitive years, years of openness and honesty, when the needs of others press close upon us. Those are years of joy and laughter, of disappointment and tears, of hope and meditation.

And those are very precious years to God. If He can weave the threads of His grace into the fabric of our youthful years, then He holds the very best. If God can harness the energy, the openness, and the soaring hopes of youth, then He can fill those wilderness years with the richness of His grace. If God can claim those years when awe and wonder are a part of everyday living, then He can create the bonds of trust that can withstand the corrosive cynicism of later years.

We dare not wait for the later years to grow up to God. The work of a Kingdom is not limited to apostles, prophets and evangelists. And older ones at that. In the hands of God, the years of our youth can be put to splendid service. Consider

David, Jeremiah, Daniel, Mark and Timothy. And the eyes of Job were opened to the power and grace of God by a young man named Elihu. Clearly the young are mighty in the hands of God. Indeed, if God can capture the years of our youth then he works with the best, and the wilderness of passing through those youthful years is eased by the certainty of his closeness, the stability of his steadfast grace.

But this wilderness of growing up is not limited to the first twenty years of our lives. In strong and subtle ways, the winds of cunning doctrine, the deceitful wiles of this world, impede our growth in grace at all stages of life. The Christian faith is always a matter of growth and begins as the Spirit of God orients our whole trust to the cross of Christ and the Christ of the cross. But as the magnetic pole must acquire the needle of a compass to permit precise navigation, so must the man of God be continuously acquired by the Spirit of God. Else he drifts, tossed to and fro by the shifting winds of temptation. Faith never really "makes it." Faith never attains. Either it grows in maturity and certainty, or it dies in carelessness. The man of God is always hungry. The grace of God creates its own hunger, and either a man feeds on God's grace or he may never attain "to mature manhood, to the measure of the stature of the fulness of Christ."

What then is the mark of Christian maturity? If it's not necessarily the visible attributes of emotional stability, insight into the difference between good and evil, and those other characteristics mentioned earlier, what *is* the mature Christian faith?

Indeed, it's the authority of God in your life that leads you out of the wilderness of growing up, that feeds your faith to maturity. You grow in faith not as you become better and better, but as you become more certain of your need for God. Not just God *in general,* but rather

God as the one central authority of the soul. You let God be *God,* and your response is to worship, trust, and obey. Christian maturity means above all else a God; we are not a cult in which we worship ourselves and our goodness.

And the supreme authority of God is of grace, not of law. He is our God not because He loves us, but because out of His love and grace He redeemed us unto Himself. The great grace is done, and God's authority rides in the cross and the Resurrection of Jesus Christ, God the Son, God of God, Light of Light, Very God of Very God. Jesus Christ is Lord and Giver of Life. By his death and Resurrection Christ is *Lord,* and as He gains His Resurrection victory in the inner chambers of your soul, He is *your* Lord and *your* God. You trust Him, and you obey the One you trust.

And thus our Lord, the Risen Christ, is the one authority that permeates all that we do and say. The lordliness, the authority of our Lord, is not a limiting, binding, shackling thing. On the contrary, He is our one source of power and strength, our true source of personal freedom. Indeed our personal freedom lies squarely in the authority of God in our lives, not in our demands for liberty. *In* Christ and *by* Christ we are truly free to speak the truth in love.

So this growing up is a matter of grace, the grace of God in Christ, the Head. *He* is our stability in times of crisis, *He* is the food that the hungry child of God feeds upon; *He* is the authority that frees us to find our brother. If God can take hold of us in our younger years, sustain us in the middle years, and comfort us in the golden years, then He has us for the eternal years.

Blessed be the God and Father of our Lord Jesus Christ! By his great mercy we have been born anew to a living hope through the resurrection of Jesus Christ from the dead, and to an inheritance which is imperishable, undefiled, and unfading, kept in heaven for you.

1 Peter 1:3–4

And hope does not disappoint us, because God's love has been poured into our hearts through the Holy Spirit which has been given to us.

Romans 5:5

Grace

In

The Wilderness:

of Hopelessness

The wilderness of hopelessness is a bleak and barren desert. When all hope is gone, when our spirits are bankrupt of courage and comfort, then like grass we slowly wither and die. The wilderness of hopelessness is filled with despair, grief, sorrow, hate and heartbreak. And in this wilderness we become lost in anger, self-pity, and suspicion. We are angry at the stranger, we will not trust our brother, we are bitter toward ourselves. The wilderness of hopelessness feeds on its own despair; it is death-ended — dead ended.

Indeed there is no hell like the wilderness of complete hopelessness. The deepest pit of hopelessness is the disappearance of God. When even God is swallowed up in our hostility and bitterness, life collapses in a pall of despair. When even God seems not to count at all, and life has no author or redeemer, darkness and desperation fill the ticking of the clock. The bell tolls only despair. With no hope in God, in my brother, in myself, the soul is hardened in cynicism and destroyed in jealousy and revenge. In the wilderness of no hope, there is no comfort, no certainty, no peace, no tomorrow.

And man can't stand that; no one can live like that? Even in the depths of grief, and despair, and hostility, and heartbreak, every heart and soul cries out for hope. Life hungers for hope, and in one way or another, you will seek a basis for it. You may search for hope in an endless round of distraction, in a relentless pace of work or pleasure, in a harsh pursuit of power, in a grand stockpiling of the wealth of this world. Or you may try to escape this wilderness by doubling the pills, popping the cork, taking a "trip."

But these exits are only sinking sand. The human heart refuses to be taken in by this fraud. Deep in the inner wells of the soul, you cry for a certain hope that rises above the distractions, the pleasure, the power, and the pills. You cry for a hope that will reach deep into your wilderness of no hope and raise you from the death of hopelessness. You seek not an escape from hard work or high responsibility, but rather you seek a certainty, a confidence, a grace that will sustain you in the midst of your troubles.

And sinking in the mire of hopelessness you turn to God, and *there, there alone,* you find your certain hope. With the writer of the Psalms you call to God: "With thy faithful help rescue me from sinking in the mire" (Psalm 69), and "My hope is in thee" (Psalm 39). You turn to God, and he is the one hope who does not disappoint you.

Hope finds its certainty in the anchorage of God. Anchored in the mud of my distractions and escape techniques, hope quickly loses its grip and runs adrift in fantasy and wishful thinking. The hope that rescues me from the wilderness of despair need be far more than wishful thinking, optimism, pie-in-the-sky, or some form of "positive thinking." The misery of the hopeless soul is far too great for human pity, human sympathy, human will power. Hopelessness needs God, or it consumes us in despair.

But hope born of God's grace does not disappoint us or consume us. Anchored in the solid rock of an Easter Resurrection, hope lives and holds firm in a world beset by despair.

In a strange way, our hope for this moment and our hope for the future lies in a mighty act of God, accomplished long years ago. In a Calvary cross of grace and in a Resurrection of victory, God imparts to human hearts a steadfast hope by the living witness of the Holy Spirit. Peter's letter ties the Christian hope squarely to the Resurrection of Jesus Christ from the dead, and Paul's letter to the Romans speaks of that hope as a "hope that does not disappoint us, because God's love has been poured into our hearts through the Holy Spirit which has been given to us." Each speaks of a past event. The incarnation of hope is done, and is born ever anew into the hearts of men as the eternal Spirit of truth turns our hearts to Good Friday and Easter. A living hope grips our hearts as the reality of a living Christ captures our faith. Life *has* its Author and Authority; life *is* redeemed; our sins *are* covered over, and the Light of the World sheds an eternal light into the wilderness of hopelessness.

Our exit from this wilderness is marked by two very significant attitudes — God's attitude to us, and ours to him. Here I speak of *grace* and *gratitude*.

Only a God of steadfast grace will lead you out of this wilderness. If you see only a God of wrath, a God of stone tablets, a God of condemnation, you will surely sink only deeper into your mire of hopelessness. When faith becomes a relationship of a living person with a Living Person, when faith is a vital communion between a son by forgiveness and a Father by grace, then hope grips your heart in a holy, unbreakable bond. As Christ lives for you, then hope dwells in you. The power that raises you from the depths of hopelessness is the full creative power of God that rides in the gospel of Jesus Christ. That *is* the grace of God at work within you, and that is your one true exit from the bleak misery of no hope.

And for that you are thankful! For the certainty and the wonder of God's unchanging grace in all that He has done for you, you respond in gratitude. You thank

Him; you praise Him; you glorify Him, and then you enjoy Him. *And you trust Him.* Out of the depths of your hopelessness, you hurl your thanks to God as you anchor your hope on His certain power. You thank Him that He has chosen to dwell among men, and you praise Him for His abiding presence. You thank Him *even for the wilderness of hopelessness that you are in.* Yes, you even thank Him for the situation, *whatever it is,* that feeds your hopelessness, your desperation, your despair.

Can you offer prayers of gratitude in the midst of hopelessness? It's not an easy thing to do. But is there not *one thing* for which you can thank God? Indeed there is. If for little else, *you can at least thank God for His grace,* for His persistent and personal love for you, for His patient searching and seeking for you, and for His power to create hope out of the wilderness of hopelessness. Out of the rubble of despair, you thank Him for His great gift of grace, and slowly, gradually new avenues of gratitude are opened, new visions of His blessings become apparent. You thank God for the big things and the little things, for life, whatever beauty you can see, the health that you do possess, for family, for friends. The stranger is not your enemy, for he is one for whom Christ died also. And your restless heart finds comfort in the certainty that God wants you, that God will never let you go. Along with the Apostle Paul, as *we* say, "Always and for everything giving thanks in the name of our Lord Jesus Christ to God the Father" (Eph. 5:20), we take our first steps out of the wilderness of hopelessness.

Grace and gratitude — these are the sure paths to a living hope. As we thank God for his grace, we are free, free from the bogs of hopelessness.

"Let not your hearts be troubled; believe in God, believe also in me. In my Father's house are many rooms; if it were not so, would I have told you that I go to prepare a place for you? And when I go and prepare a place for you, I will come again and will take you to myself, that where I am you may be also."

John 14:1–3

"I will not leave you desolate; I will come to you. Yet a little while, and the world will see me no more, but you will see me; because I live, you will live also."

John 14:18–19

Grace

In

The Wilderness:

of Death

Our passage through the wilderness of death is a lonely, lonely walk. *But by the grace of God, we do not walk it alone.* By the grace of God we may pass through this wilderness with Someone who knows the way.

In my years as a pilot in the Air Force flying transport runs, we never flew as pilot until we flew the route many times as co-pilot. During the co-pilot trips, we learned the airport layouts, the terrain characteristics, the navigation facilities, the radio frequencies, the instrument approach procedures, etc. Every detail of the route was absorbed in those trips as co-pilot. We always flew with someone who had been "there."

So it is as we move through the valley of the shadow of death. We travel with Someone who has been there — *and back again.*

And that Someone is Jesus Christ, the risen Son of God. On a Good Friday cross, He was crucified to death. On a cross at Calvary He tasted the awful wilderness of death, and if it had ended there, you and I would be left desolate in an awesome wilderness. But death could not hold Him. God raised Him from the dead, and that Easter Resurrection was God's pronouncement to the world that the cycle of life is not from life to death but from life to death to life — eternal life with God. The return of Christ from the wilderness of death is our certain assurance that even in the wilderness of death, God can create life. Into the dust of our death God again breathes eternal life. The Risen Christ is our escort through the wilderness: "I will not leave you desolate; I will come to you." At the horizon of death this same Jesus of the cross makes his rendezvous with us to take us through to God. "Because I live, you will live also." You will live with God.

It's a strange story, isn't it? Why should God deal with my death through the death and the Resurrection of Jesus Christ? Was there no other way for God to deal with the "last enemy," death?

Death raises many agonizing and haunting questions. Death is the great unknown for every man, and we are fearful and suspicious of the unknown. Death is totally irrational, and we cannot comprehend it. The bell tolls for every man, but like the twisting tornado, death's path is so unpredictable. No one knows his appointment with the last enemy, and that wilderness of death breeds questions, fear, frustration, and anger.

In the midst of these haunting questions, I can turn only to the grace *in* God to find any light at all to this dark tunnel. For in His grace I am bold to believe that *life,* not death, is the great purpose of God among men. Death is the stranger. Death is the unwelcome intruder in God's house. Death is the great embezzeler who tries to defraud us from God. Death is the fearful wedge that seeks to separate us from the heavenly Father.

But God would not settle for that. He has forever broken the power, exposed the fraud, calmed the fears, of the "last enemy."

For God Himself accepted the challenge of death. God seized upon the universality of death to pour forth the universality of His grace. He took what was common to every man — death — and transformed it into the one dominant theme of grace. On a cross at Calvary, God entered the arena of death to come to grips with its destructive power. He descended into hell, that you and I may not, and He raised Christ from death in a victory of grace. God mastered death in the wilderness of death and made of that bleak wilderness a road to glory — a road to the glory of God himself.

And so in the midst of our questions and fear and anger, there is a certain hope. Death is not the last act of the play; there is more beyond. We cannot read fully that script, but we place those acts into the directing hands of God. The questions will continue to haunt us for a lifetime, but as we turn to God in our struggles with the reality of death, we meet squarely the incredible power of his grace. In the wilderness of death, our hearts are not troubled, for we fix the eyes of faith upon that grace, and our restless hearts find certainty and confidence. Indeed, we rest in the certainty that the way through the wilderness has been *prepared* and *shared.*

". . .I go to prepare a place for you.

And when I go and prepare a place for you, I will come again and will take you to myself, that where I am you may be also." In those words of our Lord, I find supreme comfort and strength. For I am no longer a wanderer in this awesome wilderness of death. I rest in the certainty that Christ Himself will meet me as I cross that horizon and lead me through to the open arms of God. He knows the way, and *I know* He knows the way. By faith we understand.

I trust solely the preparation that Christ has accomplished for me on that cross. I cannot make adequate preparations myself. Death is the one great event in life that we cannot rehearse. We make one run through that awesome wilderness, *one only.* We do not travel the route over and over again to become familiar with its hazards. Rather we cruise the course one time, and we put our trust in the one Pilot who knows the route. He has pioneered the frontier; he has already mapped the wilderness.

But the real miracle of grace is that God shares His Easter victory over death with everyone who believes in God the Son. "Because I live, you will live also," Christ promised. In a strange way, His victory over death becomes ours, as we are drawn and held to this Risen Savior in faith. As God wins His Easter victory in the tombs of your soul, you are bound to him by a bond that neither life, nor death, nor anything in all creation can sever. "Believe in God, believe also in me," Christ said. This is God's persistent call to you to join with Him *now* in a relationship that knows no end. As you come to God with that great response of faith, "God, I believe — Christ, my Lord and my God," your course through the wilderness of death is, *right then*, established. You're heading for the Father's house of many rooms. A life with God, through faith in Jesus Christ, can never die. Your faith in Jesus Christ is the master of your death. The way is prepared, and the victory is shared. *Believe it, and you have it!*

This wilderness of death lies out ahead for all of us. None can escape it. All that you can take with you as you enter that wilderness is your faith is Jesus Christ. Everything else is left behind.

But when you walk through the valley of the shadow of death, a Savior will draw near and say, "Here, take my hand. Do not be afraid, for I know the way." The Risen Christ will come to you to take you around the bend, to dwell in the house of the Lord forever.

In the wilderness of death, God can create life. That is the certainty and the comfort of Easter Day. Christ is risen! He lives! Thanks be to God, that though the wilderness of death is a lonely walk, we do not walk it alone.

And to keep me from being too elated by the abundance of revelations, a thorn was given me in the flesh, a messenger of Satan, to harass me, to keep me from being too elated. Three times I besought the Lord about this, that it should leave me; but he said to me, "My grace is sufficient for you, for my power is made perfect in weakness."

2 Corinthians 12:7–9

Grace

In

The Wilderness:

of Your Life

The abundant grace of God is sufficient for you. The revelation of God given through God the Son is enough. In this Jesus of Bethlehem, this Christ of the cross, this Risen Lord of life, you have been given *all* that you need. He *is* the living grace of God searching and seeking you in the wilderness moments of your life.

In whatever wilderness you may wander, you are *never, never* beyond the searching, probing grace of God. It's the grand nature of grace that God will not give up on you, at least on this side of the grave. There is no hell in your life that God will not enter. The words of the Psalm writer are as true for you as for him: "If I ascend to heaven, thou art there! If I make my bed in Sheol, thou art there!" (Psalm 139:8). Whatever wilderness you may wander, God is there! You cannot shock God.

In the pages of this book, we have wandered in and out of several wildernesses — loneliness, doubt, uncertainty, suffering, guilt, procrastination, growing up, hopelessness, and death. At times you may experience one or another of these areas of darkness; at other moments, a combination of these may press upon you. Or none of these may be your wilderness today. The thorn in your flesh today that keeps driving you into the wilderness may be quite different from those we have looked at. A struggle with drugs or alcohol — perhaps these are keeping you in a bleak wilderness. Or a turbulent marriage, a prodigal son or daughter, or dreams and visions for your life that just didn't work out, a broken heart over a broken courtship, perhaps one of these may be your wilderness at this moment. *Whatever* it may be, *God — and the grace of God, are adequate for your need.*

But can you really accept that? Is this just so much holy smoke that evokes anger instead of comfort? Or do you consider that your "thorn" is far beyond the power of God?

If you seek only the removal of the thorn, you may never see the grace of God acting in and through your need. It may seem to you that God is not much concerned with the wilderness details that torment you. The pain and the heartbreak are before you, and God seems unwilling to remove them. As you plea mightily with God about a personal matter in your life, He becomes more of a burden than a God of grace, more of an object for anger than a God to worship, as the thorny details seem to pass unresolved. This apparent silence of God drives you deeper into your personal wilderness, and you trust neither God nor His grace. When He doesn't seem to "work" for you, when He fails to deliver the goods, you give up on God. You trust no one.

But are not the dimensions of God's grace far greater than our "thorns"? Is God not more concerned with perfecting His power within the framework of our weaknesses than in making life pleasurable for us? Is not every wilderness in our life there in order to arouse in us our need for God Himself? It seems that God dismissed Paul's plea for the thorn's removal. But that is not so. He seems to say: "I know your problem. I'm quite aware of your troubled life. But in your weakness — your wilderness — I want to perfect in you the overwhelming power of my grace. I want you to know that my grace is really what you need."

And the wonder is that Paul saw it God's way. ". . .for when I am weak then I am strong," he said. Paul saw in his affliction a means, a channel through which the grace of God strengthened its hold upon him.

Can you? In the wilderness of your life, can you see ever more clearly the persistent, powerful grace of God at work?

It's not an easy thing to do. It takes courage. It requires a deep trust in God. It calls for a confidence in God that not even a crown of thorns can alter.

Grace is not cheap either for God or for you. Surely God grieves over our sorrow and suffering. What father would not grieve over the suffering of a son? But is not the father more interested in maintaining the close relationship of father and son than in overcoming the son's suffering? The relationship, established in love, is absolutely primary. For if this bond of love is broken, then the father has no real access to his son. The son is lost to both the father's love and his own inheritance.

It's our human lostness that grieves our heavenly Father. Surely he grieves over our human suffering, but our drifting in the far country, far from the Father's care, is of primary concern to God. For in the thorny far country, we invariably seek the cheap grace, the quick cure, the foxhole of pleasure. In our desperate search for bigger and better pigpens, we lose sight of the Father's house.

And God would not have it that way for us. There is no cheap grace. It took a costly cross for God to convey to the hearts of men the awesome depths of His loving grace. The Son of God bled and died on a cruel Cross in order that God could treat us drifting sinners as sons. That is God's great purpose for us — to keep us in the orbit of His love and forgiveness as sons, as children of the heavenly Father. His great purpose for us is to commune with us in a living, personal, daily, eternal, holy communion of grace. And that required a Savior, a cross, and an empty Easter tomb. The grace of the cross is done; it is finished, *and that is the grace that is sufficient for you.* You seek no new and bizzare revelation of God; the grace of the cross is all that you need to keep you in the orbit of your God. The grace of God acting upon us in Jesus Christ is the greatest thing that God has ever done, and your trust in this grace is the highest thing that you can do.

As with Paul, God does not always remove the thorns that seem to make a wilderness of our lives. God does not necessarily spare us things. He is not really a bridge *over* troubled waters. Rather He seeks to create in us the certainty that He is always near to us, that we are never beyond His care and concern. He seeks to instill in us the power and the courage to move *through* the troubled waters, to make us strong when we are weak.

In our weakness, we cry to God, and he says,

"My grace is sufficient for you."

In our cry for peace, God says, "My grace is sufficient for you."

In our cry for good health, he says, "My grace is sufficient for you."

In our cry for the good life, he says, "My grace is sufficient for you."

In our cry for a generous portion of the world's wealth, he says, "My grace is sufficient for you."

In the wildernesses of our loneliness, doubt, uncertainty, suffering, guilt, procrastination, growing up, hopelessness, death, whatever wilderness you are in at this moment, God thunders again and again, *"My grace is sufficient for you."*

And that is what makes his grace so costly to us. We need to die to our self-centered thorns before we can see it, and see it as sufficient for the central issues of life and death.

Indeed the wondrous grace of God is far broader than our needs, far richer than our dreams. As we turn in trust to the abundant grace of God as poured out upon us in Jesus Christ the Lord, we say, "Thanks be to God for his inexpressible gift *of grace!* "